ABOVE AND BEYOND

poetry *pt* today

ABOVE AND BEYOND

Edited by Suzy Walton

First published in Great Britain in 2001 by Poetry
Today, an imprint of
Penhaligon Page Ltd, Remus House, Coltsfoot Drive,
Woodston, Peterborough. PE2 9JX

A Catalogue record for this book is available from the
British Library

ISBN 1 86226 643 3

Typesetting and layout, Penhaligon Page Ltd, England.
Printed and bound by Forward Press Ltd, England

Foreword

Above And Beyond is a compilation of poetry, featuring some of our finest poets. This book gives an insight into the essence of modern living and deals with the reality of life today. We think we have created an anthology with a universal appeal.

There are many technical aspects to the writing of poetry and *Above And Beyond* contains free verse and examples of more structured work from a wealth of talented poets.

Poetry is a coat of many colours. Today's poets write in a limitless array of styles: traditional rhyming poetry is as alive and kicking today as modern free verse. Language ranges from easily accessible to intricate and elusive.

Poems have a lot to offer in our fast-paced 'instant' world. Reading poems gives us an opportunity to sit back and explore ourselves and the world around us.

Contents

My Last Farewell

I love you like a daughter
You'll always be my Michelle
If only I could wish you happiness
Instead of a life of hell.
You gave me pain and sorrow
Don't hear my heartache cry
But I will always love you
Until the day I die.

Adultery you committed
With men from the Internet
Perhaps, I could be forgiving
But I certainly won't forget.
Your daughter you deserted
Destroyed your husband too
For all your evil ways
I'll never stop loving you.

How can you find happiness
At such a terrible cost?
You'll always be a loser
Just look at what you've lost.
I know the time is here
To say my last farewell
I love you like a daughter
You'll always be my Michelle.

Dennis N Davies

1

Colours In Rhyme

Red wrinkled babies
Little pink pigs
Toffee-nosed ladies
With blond and black wigs
Little green men
And little white lies
Blue is the pen
And grey are the sighs
Buttercups yellow
Daisies white
The moon is mellow
In the black of night
Cowards are yellow and so is custard
Green with envy, pass the mustard
Red with temper, white with fear
Crying a transparent tear
Red, yellow, pink, green, orange, purple, blue
These are the rainbow colours, which I give to you
Red is the beautiful sunset
Yellow the glow of the moon
Pink the dawn which perhaps you have met
And green the trees to prune
Orange flowers so bright to behold
Purple mountains their beauty unfold
But blue is the prettiest of all say I
Because God used it to colour the sky.

Roberta Ellis

The Summertime

In the summertime, at the end of the day,
I crawl into bed and pray and pray
That one tiny breeze will blow on me
Before I cease to be . . .
I peel off my clothes until I'm nude,
On top of the bed I lie, though it's rude,
Open the windows, turn on the fan,
And try to sleep as long as I can.
I'll do anything to avoid the feeling
That all my skin has started peeling.
My hair looks and feels like harvest stubble,
My throat is as dry as builders' rubble.
In my mind I imagine it's cold ~
Snow and frost have covered the road.
I just go on longing for change
To temperatures in the sub-zero range.

M J Stewart

It's A Boy

Rachel I want to thank you
For bringing us such joy,
You have made a miracle
With our beautiful baby boy.

I can't describe these feelings
That I'm feeling deep inside,
My eyes filled up with tears
Tears I couldn't hide.

Now we truly are a family
We will always be as one,
You and me and Joshua James
Our miracle baby son.

I'll always do my best for us
I'll do the best I can,
From Joshua coming home
Right through 'til he's a man.

Once again I thank you
For putting up with the pains,
A whole nine months inside you
Will you do it again?

Joshua will be a happy child
He will be our lucky charm,
We will honour and protect him
He will always be kept from harm.

Peter James Hartley

Daylight Robbery

Began work on my veggie patch I'd lately had to leave.
First task being strong with myself, was roll up both my sleeves.
Went toward the little shed where garden tools are kept.
Without those would do half a job, appearing most inept.
Looking at my strawberries ripening mid fresh hay,
Something made me hesitate before turning away.
I froze stock still and waited 'longside my tool house.
After a while small nose peeped out, its owner was a mouse.
Gently it ran across the ground to biggest berry there.
He either didn't notice me, or else he didn't care.
Nibbling through the strawberry stem once that task he'd done,
Began hard work of tugging it to where he had his home.
He and his treasure disappeared, letting it seem to me,
Whatever for his dinner'd had, fancied strawberry tea.
I'll let him have one every day and he may have it free.
Payment for delight it gave watching such *daylight robbery*.

Barbara Goode

She Smiled But Her Eyes Conveyed A Different Mood

She smiles, her eyes alive, so bright
Infectious joy she radiates
The warmth and love that she creates
Bring light into the darkest night

She smiles, her eyes inert, subdued
In vain she seeks, her mind still clear
To hide from view a crystal tear
Lest her pain be misconstrued

She smiles, her eyes intense, alert
A casual glance did not reveal
The feelings she wanted to conceal
Disguising any hurt

She smiles, her eyes awash with song
No limits to her love she knows
Transparent now her passion glows
Intoxicating, sweet and strong

She smiles, always she smiles but she
Through eyes displays a different mood
To comprehend, it's understood
First you must seek and then you'll see

Clive Reading

Ditto

Everyone wants what the other person has got,
No-one is content with their lot,
We must be one of the few,
You are happy with me, ditto me with you.

You get back what you give out,
So we have plenty to smile about,
We have our rows, of course we do,
But you are happy with me, ditto me with you.

I thank God, for how lucky we are,
More fortunate than many others it seems, by far,
It seems we have found true love, us two,
You love me, ditto me with you.

Maureen Arnold

Once Upon A Rhythm...

Sonic mastery
In the story
Of downbeat to upbeat
In word passing fleet:
From ancient dance
To serious message a glance
At the pulse
To smile or convulse
Or some might weep
In the human beat to ocean's deep.

Some say a pattern scanning
The visible to infinite planning
That equation in the plan
In disciplines and ran
A repetitive or constant alliteration
In letters or human oration,
Even the natural scene
A mathematic mystery where we preen
To know our answer only to
A new repeat to know our answers only true.

John Amsden

I Love You More

I love you more than words can say,
I love you more and more each day.
I love you more than glittering snow,
I love you more than you'll ever know.
I love you more than the sun does shine,
I love you more as I know you are mine.
I love you more than a welcoming breeze,
I even love you when you sneeze.
I love you more than diamonds and gold,
I'll even love you when we are old.
I love you more than wealth and money,
Yes, I really love you honey.
I love you more than chocolate cake,
I have so much love for you to take.
I love you more than you can see,
Me and you will always be.
I love you with all my heart,
Our hands are joined and will never part.
I love you more than the stars up high,
I'll love you till the day I die.

S L Teasdale

The Visit

In the flickering light from the fireplace,
When the curtains are tightly drawn,
Along the wall the shadows chase,
Father Christmas by reindeer drawn.

I'm sure he stopped at our chimney pot,
Snuggle under the bed-clothes, don't peep!
I left a mince pie and some tea in a pot,
Some freshly crushed oats in a heap.

How can he remember all that I want
With so many children to see?
I wrote a letter, with my name, to say
'Father Christmas, please remember me.'

I asked for a ball, a train and some sweets,
Perhaps some surprises as well,
A lucky-bag that's filled with treats,
A book full of stories to tell.

I'll close my eyes tight, snuggle under the sheets,
'Tomorrow soon comes', so they say.
No more listening now, and no more peeps,
Tomorrow is Christmas Day!

Joan Thompson

Going Home To God

When your body's trapped in slow decay
And there seems no end in view
Remember that the Lord on high
Is never far from you

Don't think that you're forgotten
That no-one seems to care
Just cast your thoughts high above
And you will find Him there

Though your body slowly weakens
And your energy is spent
Just place yourself in His hands
And you will find new strength

He's there for you every day
And if you serve Him true
You'll find the gates of heaven
Will open wide for you

Patrick Greaves

Ode To R M

I've seen you looking happy, I've seen you looking sad,
I've seen you being patient and I've seen you get 'real mad',
You sometimes make the odd mistake (but then I make some, too!)
And sometimes you just cannot see what's right in front of you.

When the pressure gets to you and you begin to panic
You give me so much urgent work I'm sure I'll end up manic;
But when I think of all the other Bosses that I've had
I reckon, with a smile, that after all ~ you're not so bad!

Pauline Geeves

A Happy Day Out

I sat and mused of times gone by
Of childhood memories which make me sigh
The days I played out in the street
With friends and playmates, always a treat
Times in the park, when we played hide and seek
Sometimes I cheated, and took a peek
A bag of sandwiches which mum had cut
A bottle of pop and a delicious jam but.
Sliding down the slide, my pants all wet
It had been raining that day, but I soon forgot
With socks around ankles, my knees red and sore
I headed for home, for mum's magical cure

Joseph Worthington

Corporal Iolo Lewis, Killed 1917

Gaza's ancient sands his footsteps have now effaced,
The desert winds have hidden the way,
That led to hell that distant day,
Eastwards the route in time encased,
Towards Jerusalem, and the foe he faced,
Where worldly faiths in distant domes obey
The need for mortals, born from clay,
And sacred words in mind embraced.

Yet then, as now, no pleasant land,
Bloody turmoil stains the arid ground.
Bones, sun-bleached, lie deeply in the sand,
To mock the faith man thought he'd found,
In this tormented strip, forever fanned
With hatred, graves old and new abound.

Tread softly round this fresh sand mound,
That hides in its tomb a noble soul,
Still your fevered pulse, as tears unroll,
In grief for Iolo in this sad surround.
Peaceful in life, let no unseemly sound,
In death his feelings stir; on glory's scroll
His honoured name in worldly terms extol,
That we his footsteps may trace through hallowed ground.

Mark well his path whereon his feet were bent
Peace for the oppressed of the earth he sought,
Duty the keynote of his life well spent,
Selfless in aim, the final deeds he wrought,
God has reclaimed what in trust he'd lent,
That he life's crown might gain, who nobly fought.

Iolo Lewis

Side Effects

Oh these pills have side effects
Yet still can cure my ills
But if I feel like I am walking on air
Is there anybody out there who cares.

Oh these pills have side effects
But they are never bad
They just give me ideas
About things I have never had.

Oh these pills have side effects
They say some others are the best
But I quite like these thank you
Now I have put them to the test.

Keith L Powell

The Twilight Hour

How lovely in these days of stress and strife,
To leave behind all the problems of modern life,
The rumbling of rushing traffic in busy street,
As we hurry along on tired and aching feet

To relax in the time between day and night,
The witching hour, known as twilight,
The harshness of nature with beauty endowed,
All forms appearing in a mystic shroud

In country lane, traffic hum a distant sound,
Where scented hedge blossom and wild flower abound,
Damp spiders' webs, all glistening white,
Show their delicate tracery in the misty twilight

Silhouette of buildings in the fading light,
Soon to vanish with the coming of night,
Stark outline of a lightning-struck tree,
A giant figure in torment, struggling to be free

How kind to the vision is this time of day,
Giving everything a look, transient and fey,
This bewitching time in the twilight hour,
Revives the tired spirit like rain to a flower

E Kathleen Jones

16

What A Car

Splutter and bang
Hey what a noise
This damn er car
Is worse than the boys
Them drunken err card sharks
And boozy louts
Have lent me this car
To take the missus out
Hope she won't mind
When she sees all the string
It's what works the engine
And the whole darn thing
Here she comes
In her best pretty dress
If I just smile and nod
She mightn't notice the rest
Off comes the door
In the palm of her hand
Should I laugh or now cry
I chose not a sound
'Boy that sure is a pretty dress
Sorry about the heap
But the lads did reassure me
They bought it real cheap.'
She smiled and said, 'Honey
I love you even more.
But I asked for a bracelet
Not a bloody car door.'

Abigail Edna Jones

Chocolate Drop!

Do *you* like chocolate pudding? Oh I love it so I do
And if I drop it down my front it sticks there just like glue!
Then if it's on the table and I dabble it around
And push my fingers in my mouth it's tastier I've found!
Now if I put my sticky hands into my nice clean hair
It gums it all together and drives mummy to despair!
She doesn't understand that chocolate isn't just to eat
And keeps on trying to wash it off to make me clean and neat.
But I *do* like chocolate pudding and tomorrow dinnertime
I'll scream and scream until I get that chocolate sublime.
It's really all I want to eat, not veg and stuff like that
But I'm sure my *mum* has tumbled to the fact I'm getting fat.
So I think my days are numbered, she won't buy me any more,
But if she gives me stuff like veg ~ I'll throw it on the floor!
Then Scamp, my lovely doggy friend who's never far away
Will come and eat up every bit ~ and I'll have won the day!

Paddy Jupp

A Heavenly Scene

On a starlit night, I gaze in utter rapture,
As those myriad stars so bright, my mind totally encapture.
Their brilliance and beauty surpass all imagination
And each constellation, proves an inspiration.
How gorgeous to witness heaven's vault alight
And view that sea of glimmering delight.
For me such a scene, is an infinite pleasure
As heaven unfolds its eternal treasure.

Helen Allan

A Rhyme In Time

I tried my hand at poetry
but wasn't very good
because I could not make them rhyme
the way I knew they might.

I had problems with the verses
some were far too short
other verses were too long
because I had a very bad habit of trying to fit far too many words in
to one line.

My spelin was also pretty pour
espesally with big words
so I usaly did not use them
unless it was compleetily and uneqivekibly nesisiry.

So this wee poem your readin
will be my very last
I know it will be just as poor
as my efforts in the past.

Hold on just a moment.
Did that last verse rhyme?
Yes it did, just look back to
the second and last line.

Good God I don't believe it,
that one rhymed as well.
Maybee I'm improving.
It's realy hard to tell.

There's something going on here
I really am quite moved,
not only are they rhyming but
my spelling has improved.

I now feel I can call my self
a Poet ~ don't you know
so I'm going to writ another one.
Goodbye and aurovwa.

George Burns

Sloth

Awakening on a Sunday morn with frost lacing the glass
And knowing that you should arise and go to morning Mass
But snuggling under warm duvets with eyes still full of sleep
The slothful says (just to himself) 'I expect the Church will keep.'

The Housewife, sitting drinking tea, surveys the mess all round
Of children's toys and clothes and books, and makes a rueful sound
'Even if I clear it up,' she thinks with slothful horror
'I just can't see what good 'twould do, 'twill be just the same
                                                    tomorrow.'

And surveying the heap of dirty clothes her family has divested
Her conscience now is pricking her, she knows she's being tested
Her slothful side is telling her, 'To hell with boys and men,
If I wash their ruddy clothes today, they'll just get black again.'

Father gazes through the glass at weeds and grass knee high
And thinks that he'll go fishing whilst the weather's nice and dry
His slothful mind is telling him that even if most men
Would cut the ruddy grass down ~ 'twould only grow again.

We all know that bread is the staff of life, indeed
We cannot live without it, it's become a must, a need
But at the local bakery, the Boss, fed up with sloth
Said, 'It doesn't mean the life of this staff should be one
                                                    continual loaf!'

So what's to do about it them, should laziness take over
And say, 'To hell with everything' and live like sheep in clover
Or should our better selves evolve and do the things we ought
Knowing well that if we skive, there's no doubt we'll be caught!

G K (Bill) Baker

22

Why? Why? Why?

Why aren't clouds blue instead of white?
Why aren't stars black at night?
Why is the sun red instead of green?
Why doesn't the postman 'gone' instead of 'been'?

Why aren't violets pink instead of blue?
Why aren't babies old instead of new?
Why is the rain wet instead of dry?
Why doesn't the sparrow swim instead of fly?

Why aren't flowers black instead of white?
Why aren't tights loose instead of tight?
Why is the sea salt instead of fresh?
Why doesn't the lion eat peas instead of flesh?

Why aren't toffees sour instead of sweet?
Why aren't feet hands and hands feet?
Why is the grass green instead of red?
Why doesn't the foot wave instead of tread?

Why aren't apples square instead of round?
Why aren't skies found underground?
Why is the snow cold instead of hot?
Why doesn't the cotton tack instead of knot?

Why aren't sponges hard instead of soft?
Why aren't cellars in a loft?
Why is the kitten weak instead of strong?
Why doesn't the sinner do right instead of wrong?

Why do I ask these question of my dad
   I drive him and my mum
      completely
         mad!

   G Carpenter

Happy Conclusions

I get restless and fazed till my rhymes come right,
Mind searching, in turmoil far into the night.
It's a challenging test of word matchability,
Which may only be solved by my rehash facility.

A new word to rhyme with, may kick-start my momentum,
So ideas can flow free again, just as I meant them.

I'm happily hooked along the lines just stated,
But in retrospect find it a bit over-rated.

When I try to switch styles to blank verse for a change
I find rhyme avoidance most hard to arrange.

Oh! But what does it matter?
I'm not writing for money!
I just treasure the pleasure of being rhymy and funny!

Clive Robson

The Rustic Lad

I have never loved the busy towns
    with their hustling bustling days
I am at heart a country lad
    born to the rustic ways
I was brought up to a country life
    amongst the wild woods and the heather
I've climbed many a mountain peak
    in fair or stormy weather
I have seen the eagle in majestic flight
    fly like an arrow through the air
Then swooping down to make a kill
    on a hapless mountain hare
I've seen the cascading mountain streams
    in foaming frothy spate
I've heard them thunder on the rocks
    as they roar and reverberate
I can name most of the wild flowers
    which in clusters all abound
They make a lovely rustic scene
    with their beauty all around.

Lachlan Taylor

Stepping Out For Fortune

We stepped out in the September air,
Full of zeal and without a care,
On our way to learn of bull and bear
And of Chinese walls, my dear.
We were going to learn how, as a pear
Drops off a tree, the place where
Fortunes are made out of thin air
Really exists, is really there.
My! How it was in my hair,
The roaring bull, the groaning bear.
We were for fun, not for fear,
And pressure was on not to scare
Easily, but to sport our non-euro lire.
We were setting out for vanity fair
And trusted our options would be clear.
We didn't want to lose on our bear
Tendency and so leave our purses bare.

R S A Bibby

One Hundred Million White Turtle Doves

You are with me every day
The love you gave me will not go away

I cannot stop thinking of you and what it would be like
To be held in your arms caught like a fishing line catches a pike

I guess I will never find out how good it feels to hold you
All I want is to be near you, feel you and hear your heartbeat all
night through

It scares me to feel like this so virgin and new
My wish is that you feel it too

You say live your life be free
But how can I when your love has got a hold on me?

I have nothing to offer you except my love
One hundred million white turtle doves

As the ocean meets the sky, the waves crash on the shore
All I can picture is us making love on the floor

Amanda Jayne

Maybe Next Time

A letter came through the post
From *Penhaligon Page*,
Requesting poems that would rhyme
They were at the judging stage,
Send in a poem, maybe I should,
Would it be good enough?
Before I typed it out finally
I would jot it down in rough.

What should it be about? I pondered,
What subject would come to mind,
Would I be inspired?
And a suitable subject find,
I thought and thought for hours
But my mind remained a blank,
I'd never get another poem published
And be unable to swank!

So to the folks at *Penhaligon*
An ode I could not write,
I thought and thought, and ended
Just sitting up all night!
So maybe next time I'll be lucky,
I'll write one of my better rhymes,
And get myself together
And manage just thirty lines!

Win Barton

Hallowe'en, A Night Of Excitement

Busy all afternoon preparing and baking cakes
Working hard for the children's sakes
They come from the neighbourhood all around
The street alive with the sound
Of children knocking on doors collecting treats
Masked and painted faces hoping for nuts and sweets
By seven o'clock the October evening is dark
Children out pretending they're monsters and witches, having a lark
Hallowe'en night, excitement fills the air
The door continually knocked, hoping I'll be there
To hand out my iced cakes of notoriety
Showing me their disguises and letting me see
How clever they are at acting out the part
Grown-ups laughing with them, everyone in good heart
I love to see the old and the young
Enjoying themselves and having fun
There's not enough laughter heard these days
But young children have such beguiling ways
Every year I look forward to this night
To see their happy faces aglow with delight.

Ann McAreavey

A Male Doubts About Heaven . . .

As I look back in time
And remember the many,
Marie and Ted, Donald and Jenny,
All gone ahead to lay the carpet?
Or hang around, just dusting and cleaning
So that when I arrive it's all sparkling and gleaming.

Maybe it's wrong, and there is no hereafter,
No heavenly space full of good grace
With female form angels floating around
In right flimsy garments not making a sound.
What happened to male angels?
Perhaps they're unworthy?

That surely cannot be the reason!
We men do our best to live the good life,
Look after our children, not beat our wife,
Let her choose the tele and watch all the soaps,
Except of course in the real football season,
When our chosen team is full of good hopes.

Is there room in heaven for those gone before?
Will we be met by long queues of ancestors
Hundreds, even thousands, of years of waiting
To see the results of mating, and mating and mating.

Perhaps heaven isn't as good as we're told.
The whole place too crowded, most people old;
Queue for a beer for hour after hour,
No AA to call on when gossamer wings
Are failing to lift when we've been on a binge.

Female angels acting as they did on earth
Ordering we males from the day of our birth,
First mother, then teacher, girlfriend and sweetheart,
Wife, mother-in-law, even our daughter.
Women and women and women and women
Who loved us to death but gave little quarter.

Edgar Wall

Jesus

Thousands and thousands of years ago.
Jesus had arrived.
King Herod had ordered all children to be slaughtered.
But luckily. Jesus survived.
When Jesus grew up. He started to preach.
He also healed the sick.
Some people believed, but some did not.
They thought it was all just a trick.
He had twelve apostles. That helped him to preach.
But one of them was to betray.
Jesus knew who it was going to be.
And he also knew on which day.
He asked them together. For one final meal.
Then he told Judas to leave the room.
He knew that Judas was the man to betray him.
And shortly he would meet his doom.
Jesus was taken and later was sentenced.
In which he was to be crucified.
He was hung on a cross with thorns in his head.
Where he suffered and later. He died.

Stephen Hibbeler

A Loveable Pet

You started life a scruffy little mite,
You scratched, riddled and sometimes bite.
To get your coat clean and bright,
I had to bathe you every other night.

You often caught birds or a mouse,
Sometimes brought them into the house.
Most nights you curled up by the fire,
Dreaming of your heart's desire.

All your food with others you'd share,
And for other kittens you would care.
You'd catch a young rabbit for your tea,
Calling the kittens to come and see.

For nineteen years you I did groom,
Now we have no long fur in the room.
You left your earthly body here below,
As your lovely spirit had somewhere else to go.

Our favourite pet we would never give away,
But your time was up and you could not stay.
And now in cat's heaven on cushions you just rest,
We miss you Furnie, you were one of the best.

Margaret Upson

Your Beauty

Do not conceal your radiant eyes,
The starlight of serenest skies.
Yet wanting of their heavenly light,
They turn to choose endless night.
Do not conceal your golden hair,
Those silken curls so soft and fair.
The sweet smell of your fragrant scent,
Your breath which to all flowers you've lent.
Do not conceal your heavenly voice,
Which makes the hearts of Gods rejoice.
With music hearing no such thing,
The nightingale forgets to sing.
Do not conceal your beauty or grace,
That's either in your mind or face.
Lest virtue overcomes by vice,
Make men believe there's no paradise.

Elisabeth Dill Perrin

Widower

With leaden stride he enters in his halls
and hears the heedless stirrings of the cat,
the hollow echo of his slow footfalls
and the bickering budgie's fitful chat.

Littering the mat, lie scattered letters;
not greetings from some dear and distant one,
but anonymous commercial matters,
or missives to some tenant long since gone.

The heavy silence of the empty street,
fills chastened rooms that want their mistress' care.
And the dripping tap's perpetual beat
pats passing time on pots and plates piled there.

Not the aroma of some homely fare,
or the grate, grinning in its homely hue.
Only the faint, stale savour of the air
pervades the chill no furnace could subdue.

So, brooding in his long accustomed place,
he dwells upon each still and empty chair
as dark deliberations fill each space
with spectres of the friends that once were there.

And when the lone, eternal day is done,
long eve and even longer night must close.
Then in his bed half-burdened now by one,
in dreams unblessed: his restless soul's repose.

Steve J Waterfield

Penrith's Golden Days

Oh how I miss those golden days;
Life was better in every way.
A quiet life for all of us.
In one another we could trust.

Here in our town what can we do?
Passages and walls are used as loos;
Take-away litter lies on the ground;
To catch the culprits, no-one's around.

The people in power have lost touch.
For our town they don't do much;
With Sunday opening for the club,
Why not turn the Church into a pub?

Are there no churchmen to be seen
To keep the Sabbath as it's always been,
A visit to Church, then have a talk,
Then after dinner go for a walk.

Oh what great times we all had
Around the fireside with mam and dad,
Laughing and joking, stories were told;
It's lovely to remember now that I'm old.

Nothing can beat the golden days;
We'd no boredom or stress in any way;
We walked around not being scared,
For one another we showed we cared.

Now to walk in the streets day or night
Here in this town, it gives us a fright,
For there's no-one about who cares
To come to your aid; they do not dare.

If only we could change our ways,
Go back in time about six decades.
What heavenly days we all had then
When everything closed by half past ten.

Five to midnight the dance closed down,
We made our way quietly home through town,
Straight up Townhead and then to bed;
No noise, no mess and little said!

I know it will never be the same.
There is no-one to take the blame.
Late night opening is here to stay.
Oh how I miss those golden days.

Francis Allen

Battling On

Tell me the effort is worthwhile
    However daunting on the way
Your needs must go the extra mile
    Bearing such setbacks come what may
For not in vain you will succeed
    To reach your goal in time of need.

'Tis when the uphill task is done
    Though weary limbs call out for rest
Journeying and pressing on
    Achieving and at times sore-pressed
In retrospect let none gainsay
    There was no struggle on the way.

Sometimes when sudden want appears
    No help at hand and on your own
Forced to accept in spite of fears
    Yet knowing you are all alone.
Go battle on, you will prevail
    Against all odds and never fail.

    Reg James

Castles

My wife is fond of castles
With drawbridge, moat, and tassels,
Whilst I, in deep depression,
Just question her obsession.
Do the ancient men of Harlech
Keep fit by chewing garlic?
And those who dwell in Bamburgh
Like buildings planned by Vanburgh?
Do those Norman hordes in Battle
Indulge in tittle-tattle?
And the Romans still in Dover
Enjoy a quick make-over?
Are the ancients up in Alnwick
A trifle strange and manic?
Does the Queen Mum up in May
Gather nuts throughout the day?
And the Queen in old Balmoral
Is her coat-of-arms quite floral?
Do the old-uns there in Warwick
Have skulls that look like Yorrick?
Do those in southern Corfe
Feel a little bit browned orf?
Are the residents in Glamis
Quite often up in arms?
And the Welsh in old Caernarfon
Do they all look thin and starvin'?
I get in huffs and hassles
Over all these blinkin' castles,
And, in bed with sad despair,
Dream of castles in the air!

Jack Scrafton

The Birds Aren't Singing Anymore

Some tears fell on death's icy hand,
As a crimson stream embraced the desert's golden sand.
The sun's healing rays of light soon vanish in this place,
As darkness builds a kingdom to hide death's gruesome face,
The beautiful thoughts of a dreamer have lost their healing power,
Yet beauty hopes in vain that there'll be an eleventh hour.
So much destruction cuts far deeper than a knife,
As death lurks in the shadows to claim another life,
And the birds aren't singing anymore, they will not make a sound,
Because they know a poet is lying dead upon the ground.

Maurice Cardwell

Closing Time

Rat-a-tat-tat on the headboard fingers
Slap bare bottom by the fireside giggles
Machine tool grinds in the factory Churchills
It's closing time

Wheatfield drives roadsides picnicking
Sparrows, poplars, broad bean picking
African adventure tripping
It's closing time

Tink-oo tink-oo turns the sky blue Viva
Home brew fuels another Christmas cracker
'It's only money you can't take it with yer!'
It's closing time

Tuesday nights with the boys Bulls Heading
Proud Dad o' two made two plus seven
Years six five with your sweetheart wedded
It's closing time

Before or since no-one I've met
Is more a shining testament
To what by gentleman is meant
It's closing time

With belly laughs and twinkling eyes
You are remembered through our lives
It's closing time so glasses high
Grandad, Pop, goodbye

Simon Whitworth

An Irish Yale

And whom shall ever should return
be it their face in the sun burn
A grave a stake awaking upon
the grass the living and all gone
Tear hills and chains away and never
the splits and shakes a barren forever
The sky upon its humble clouds in awe
Not a soul a flake in flaw
No thoughts no wrong in eyes spike
One dream no dream just fight

And whom shall ever should breakdown
be it a whisper and never a sound
Never a shine upon ears of any
She's gone and seen my Irish Granny
What I will see go on; like many
And on and on; no dream just fight
bound for eagle's wings; A life of night . . .
A triumph be good no troy
just a father whispering on his knee his boy

And whom shall ever would shout and see
Who they be ~ One dream, and one key

Anita Branagan

42

Human Race

There has to be a better place,
Far away from this human race,
Too much killing, too much hate,
Greed and poverty all over the place.
Children need direction,
Always require attention,
Loving parents to listen
And understand.
Stop fighting, stop shouting,
Keep loving intentions at hand,
With a smile to cheer,
Arms wrapped around.
Warmth and love found
For a frightened child.
They find no reason to hide
From this human race.
Communication, not discrimination
For our children of this generation.

Rosemary Sheridan

The Bothie

Here in this humble bothie,
Where whisky's not grown stale or beer frothy,
Where the peat fire flames grow higher and higher,
And all is quiet in the byre,
No women here to vent her ire,
When all I desire is all I desire,
Someone, somewhere plays their moothie,
When all is cosy, all is couthie,
The moothie like a gypsy violin,
Welcome stranger and come in,
We'll open a bully-beef tin,
Peace and quiet,
No din,
You can have a piece of cream cheese,
And you can do just what you please,
And in the firelight's dying ember,
Takes me back to people and places I remember,
And in this simple but and ben,
As if by magic,
Faces and characters appear I used to ken,
Some humorous, some tragic,
I'm tired now and feeling lethargic,
Night birds call in syncopation,
As I fall asleep pondering the fate of the Scottish nation.

Alan Pow

Smiles

Walking along the road
Wearing a smile on my face,
Brings out other people's
From their secret hiding place.

To look them in the eye
With an air of surprise,
And get a smile in return
That is worthy of a prize.

To see people wrinkled with age
At bus stops, with closed up faces,
To smile with cheerful greeting
Can lift those well-worn grimaces.

Little children will return your smile
But with a certain look of doubt,
Having been taught by parents
To be careful throwing smiles about.

The best smiles come with joy
From one you love and cherish,
Who are happy to see you
And to hug you is their greatest wish.

Edwin W Branagan

The Cult

Osbert de Fyle was a loner who longed to be a leader:
An inadequate dreamer who yearned for the trappings of power.
    He founded a cult
    With the happy result
That a commune soon flourished ~ disciples joined up by the hour.

For Osbert possessed a mystique ~ a persuasive charisma ~
That captured the spirit of those who would answer his call.
    He offered them healings
    And mystical feelings.
They responded with wholesale surrender, and gave him their all.

He used the technique he had learnt from the Law and the Prophets:
The rules he laid down must be followed and strictly obeyed.
    As some of his preaching
    Agreed with Christ's teaching
The commune supposed that their ticket to Heaven had been paid.

But alas! If the motive is not to give Jesus the glory,
Then other base elements find they may share the control.
    Soon Satan was sending
    His imps of mind-bending:
The pride, greed and lust which were Osbert's took over his soul.

When Osbert had ruined the lives of some hundreds of persons
They remembered the rule which the Lord had advised them to keep:
    Beware false deceivers
    Who trap unbelievers:
They are ravening wolves who rise up in the garments of sheep.

Simon Peterson

Healing Revelations

Gently kissed by a guardian angel I might well have been,
The splendorous transformation can so clear-sightedly be seen,
Yet much more gladsomely ~ and doubtless you'll agree
That despite the muscular ataxic debility,
Affecting the postural balancing ability
In addition to the underfoot's painful soles constancy
An inner strength, that's heaven sent, prevailing from above
Is much alike being on a spiritually uplifting adventure,
    ~ A guideforce tour
Graciously empowered with blessings, from God's infinite love

Eleanor Haydon Sanderson

Winter Solstice

The window mirrors a collage of shapes:
Ghosted fragments, patterned with crystal glints;
A silenced music, the ear sips and drinks,
The garden beyond it ~ mildewed December,
Before snowfall, something that sleeps and waits.
The Father flows into the Son, and us,
Making Sons of God, as if his work once done,
Was not complete, until it included all;
As if this garden was a waiting Eden,
Without the fall, without the serpent curled
About the Tree of Life, watching for Eve's return,
Or was the April garden's daffodil life
Echoed in us, where the eternal is furled
In every leaf; and being nothing, we're loved.

Alan C Brown

The Fight

A bloke come in the bar last night,
And managed to provoke this guy to fight,
He threw a left and the other a right,
As all bystanders ran for cover outa sight,
Blood was spilt with broken glass,
As the pugilist fought over the other guy's lass,
Eventually the latter gave such a clout,
That knocked the former down and out,
Sore red with rage and beaten blue,
He now has bruises of amethyst hue.

Anthony John Ward

Harry The Bull

Harry the bull was unhappy!
He looked in the mirror and cried!
'I'm a freak ~ I've no udder
It's due to my mother
She's missed something off of my hide.'

He went out to graze
Then he rolled in the mud
And up in the hedge he espied
A glove made of rubber
It looked just like an udder
'I've found one ~ it's just the right size.'

He leapt to his hooves
Jiggled the hedge with his horns
And the glove fluttered down to the ground
'I'll fill it with sand
Strap it round with a band
It will be the best udder around!'

After a year and a day
He was grazing away
When into his field came another
She was gorgeous and round
With soft eyes of brown
She looked very much like his mother!

She fluttered her lashes
And gave him a wink
'Hello ~ what's your name?'
He said, 'Harry.'
She said, 'That's a surprise'
And looked into his eyes
'Perhaps one day soon we could marry?'

They floated away
And fed every day
On oysters, chocolate and laughter
They made love and they sang
His udder went bang
And they lived happily ever after.

J M Carpenter

Thunderstorm
(This poem is especially for Rachel)

She stuck her finger in her ear
In a bid not to hear
The rumbling, rolling battle
Of each pealing thunderous rattle.

She hid her head beneath the sheet
In a bid not to greet
The blinding blue flash of light
That came to ruin her sleep that night.

She tried so hard to be brave
Then ran, so mum's bed could save
Her from that dreadful storm
To peacefully sleep until the morn.

Sarah A P Gallagher

The Weather Forecast

'Sunshine and bright intervals are forecast today'
The television newscaster went on to say
'And it will remain warm for the rest of the day'
It all looks so promising on his colourful display

The symbols change and next day is shown
'By this time tomorrow cold rain will be blown'
This is a forecast we cannot condone
'All of it's rubbish, tell him to go home!'

The map disappears and he vanishes from view
He did seem so charming but he hasn't a clue
It's pouring outside and there's a dark overcast hue
He was reading out yesterday's now completely untrue

Keith B Osborne

Elizabethan Lament

Oh! Silver moon arising, in the velvet night,
Chase away the shadows, put the clouds to flight.
Paint a way of light across the midnight sea,
A path to bring my loved one sailing back to me.
Let your moonbeams dance, across the rippling bay,
Lighting up my footsteps as if it were the day.
Let me see my way across this lonely sand
To watch if his ship is sailing in to land.
Hear my lonely sighs, Oh! Goddess of the night,
Bathe all my world with your pure silver light.
Keep the ghosts of night away, until the break of day
Tints the sky with pink and gold all along the bay.
Elizabeth his queen wants more and more new land.
I want him home and safe upon the sand.
Years he's been off sailing upon the mighty main,
Let me see his ship come home at last again.
'Ere another evening turns to night once more,
Let me see the longboat bring him into shore.
Before you rise again across the midnight sea,
On your journey, silver moon, listen to my plea.

Haidee Williams

Tell Your Troubles To The Wind

Tell your troubles to the wind.
Blow away those cobwebs, and clear the mind.
Talk to the spirit . . .
If of course, you believe in it!

Voices of my loved ones, long departed this life.
Help me through troubled times and strife.
They often send me a sign, to show me I'm not alone.
It may be a feather or just a stone.

Many years ago, one thing did amaze me.
It was proof, I was meant to see.
One dark winter's night the wind did blow
a gift from spirit, my long lost black lace hair bow!

Its whereabouts I'd often wondered.
Above my head it hovered.
Like an autumn leaf silently floating.
I reached out and caught it . . .trembling!

It was only a simple thing,
a far greater treasure than a diamond ring.
That black lace bow meant a lot to me,
When I wore it, I felt like a true Romany gypsy.

Deidre Maria West

Electoral Role

The election bandwagon is back in town,
Greeted by smiles, yet many a frown.
The loyal, the certain, also the unsure,
Will now be targeted for the knock on the door.
Characters will be blackened, and promises made,
You do not cultivate a garden, without first using a spade.

Yet is our democracy like sun after cloud,
Or is it empty, like the undertaker's shroud?
Votes are counted in an environment secure,
Though if they really counted, it would mean much more.

T J Dean

Time

The heavy hands of Time stand still
Like the grinding wheels of a watermill
Where drought has starved it of its need
To function smoothly, flow with speed.

Each droplet precious to its aim
To reach its goal and movement gain.
Like Time is holding back reserve
To grasp each moment to preserve

This perfect setting locked in time
Enchanting feelings, so sublime.
No fear, no sound, the scent of dill
Let heavy hands of Time stand still.

Eleanor Magee

Siren Of Dreams

Let me hold you tonight
My Queen of the North
With a passion devoid
Of the seeds of remorse
Awake to the dawn when the ghosts of your past
Glide silently backwards
Away from your grasp
Hold hope by the hand
In your quest to be free
Of the shackles that bind you
And keep you from me.

Let me hold you tonight
My siren of dreams
The beauty within you
Your face so serene
Stirs my desires in a maelstrom of hope
That one day you'll realise
The words that I wrote
Were of feelings so real
As the moon up above
Surrounded by stars
In a heart full of love

J De Sola Pinto

The Circle Of Life

A furrowed brow with expanse of life exposed
And such saddened eyes with vision dimmed with age,
As he sits alone with nothing but repose
Life's circle almost completed, the last stage.

An innocent babe he came into the world
The circle of life for him then began,
The banner of existence slowly unfurled
Not apparent, the years, his life would then span.

With love and attention, signs of devotion,
This beautiful babe being nurtured with care
And from early signs he focused attention
On musical sounds as they captured the air.

Then gently, forward, he began to travel,
With strength ever growing he was making his mark,
At every hurdle he tried not to stumble
And ability grew as light shines from a spark.

As a young man love of music appearing
Melodious sounds his fingers producing
From ivory keys, a delight to the hearing
His future now certain, a talent convincing.

His fame as a conductor was slowly growing
He then married for love and happiness grew,
His future and fortune were sealed by the feeling
Of love for his wife and children, so true.

But alone he sits with fingers entwining,
His children elsewhere as he grieves for his wife,
Unfocused attention without feeling,
Now almost completed, 'The Circle of Life.'

Irene Grahame

59

Let There Be Rhyming Times

There is a right time to rhyme
When life is full of sublime
Thoughts, that brighten one's life
From day to day, one can hide from constant strife

It is good to be alive
When shadows are cast aside
And divine love finds its proper place
As lovers steal moments of ideal grace

Keep well designed thoughts at bay
It's sure to be the right way
Do not let your heart be still
Use the art of rhyming at will

Be of good cheer rhyming time is happily here
The time to rhyme promises there
Will be great moments of bliss
We lovers of words do not ever want to miss

So, here's to the rhyming time glory
Just a moment's throw away, will be a story
Of rhymes that come to stay
Through perfect happiness each hour of the day

Alma Montgomery Frank

Laughter In Heaven

I went to the funeral of a friend
We had the service, and then after
I saw lots of men beside a coach
Absolutely racked with laughter
Howling, shrieking with tears abound
Arms supporting one-another,
Sinking to the ground

I went up to a podgy bloke
And politely asked, 'What is the joke?'
He tried three times to answer me
But his tie was caught beneath his knee
He stumbled up and with a grin
Said, 'You won't believe the state we're in.'

Their work-mate Bill had passed away
They'd hired the coach out for the day
The factory closed in anticipation
Of going to London for Bill's cremation
Arriving with only seconds to spare
To find that they should not be there.

To the wrong crematorium they had come
But said that Bill would have enjoyed the fun
He was a practical joker all his life
Was much loved by his long-suffering wife
Everyone said he was a lovely bloke
And Heaven would be rocking at his latest joke!

Rose Horscroft

61

Busker On Penny Lane

Jingle-jangle played the guitar man ~
strumming a song ~ he's a Beatles fan.
Singing 'Sergeant Pepper's Lonely Hearts Club Band',
on Penny Lane he would always stand.
It's summertime, so he's got a tan.

It's hot, a drop of sweat down his cheek ran;
he smiled, wiped his cheek ~ then he began.
'Paperback Writer' is in big demand ~
    Jingle-jangle . . .

He played a medley, 10 minutes its span ~
but 'Strawberry Fields' wasn't in the plan.
Admirers shout, 'I wanna hold your hand',
and his clinging wife doesn't understand.
He loves his guitar, and the way she can
    Jingle-jangle . . .

O Phillips

The Ballad Of Strike Action

The die was cast so be it then
The little straw had weight enough
As grim of visage out walked the men.
For the motion had called for strong rebuff.

The management to a meeting hie'd
And in their wisdom laid off more
Till office and factory almost died
Few then indeed went through the door.

On worldly stage the disputation
Was carried to ministerial head
That sage considered the situation
Whilst latest comic cuts he read

'Brothers,' said he, 'I'll need more time
'Twill take for me at least three weeks
Return to that sunny eastern clime
Whilst giving your belts another tweak.'

Convenor then called a further meeting
To give the faithful all the news
That whilst ministerial cogs were creaking
All brothers must tighten up their trews

So back once more to home and castle
To wifely lists of chores undone
From masters slave to spouses vassal
Gone sweet thoughts of strolls in sun

Worse now by far than trial by jury
Or Foreman daily threatening life
Now hourly with much greater fury
There's no respite from a nagging wife.

John Wilkinson

Time Rules!

In these days as we rush about,
Time is important, there's no doubt.
Appointments fill each working day ~
'I'm late, I know, I'm on my way!'

We watch the clock from morn to night,
Some timepiece never out of sight:
Our diaries crammed with dates to keep
As soon as we awake from sleep.

But stop a moment, spare a thought
For timepiece of a different sort:
A sundial, elegant on lawn,
In days before the clock was 'born'.

No nagging ringing of the phone,
No E-mails urgent in their tone,
No striking clock to mark the hours,
No stressful lifestyle that is ours.

A time when life moved at a pace
That wasn't constantly a race
To fit in yet another chore
Before we stop for tea at four.

The daily round in days gone by
Was ruled by sun up in the sky
As shadows slowly moved around,
No strident, electronic sound!

And early man's inventive mind
Having not yet a clock to wind
Marked passing hours a simple way ~
A candle, notched, marked hours each day.

Throughout our lives time has its place,
From birth to death it sets the pace,
But I must not allow the time
To stop me finishing this rhyme!

   Roma Davies

The Raging Storm

Howling gales and slashing rain
A lightning flash in the country lane
Cannons of thunder, winds whistle and sigh
Inky black clouds overshadow the sky
A giant oak at the end of the lane
With a bearing of pride, will be never the same
By a lightning fork its branches torn
Robbed of its glory in a violent storm
Burrowing creatures each one in a hurry
Home to their shelter they scuttle and scurry
Hedgerows are stripped, their foliage torn
Wet and dejected, a sad field of corn
Bushes and leaves are tossed in the air
Down in the meadow a little grey mare
Seeks warmth and protection to keep her from harm
Frightened and lonely in the grip of the storm
The battering wind in a restless mood
Rides over the lane and into the wood
There havoc to cause with its powerful lash
To the growth in the forest that stands in its path
Restless by nature he turned to the town
Where windows are bolted and shutters pulled down
With his stormy companions, they all rage through the sky
Slates sail from a roof and chimney pots fly
Whipping up waters murky and dank
To flood in the street from a burst river bank
Their energy spent, with never a thought
For the wanton destruction the four of them wrought
They are off to their rest ~ had a strenuous day
Leaving plunder and pillage as they all fade away.

Barbara Davies

Tick Tock

The clock on the wall is ticking away,
Its seconds, its minutes, all through the day.
It is ticking away your time on earth,
The years allocated at the hour of your birth.
Your life is a story and as the chapters unfold
Each age has its part till the story is told.
And as in memory you re-read this tale
The episodes amaze you ~ how did you prevail?
Your years have been spent and now you take stock.
And the clock goes on ticking,
Tick tock, tick tock.

A M Miller

The Threes Phenomenon

They say bad luck comes in threes
This appears to be the case,
Like waiting on a certain bus
At the wrong time, in the wrong place.

First to start the proceedings off
Was a lady who should've known better,
Her accident and resulting broken wrist
Is well documented in a *'Clinton'* letter.

Next to comply under the 3's rule
Was a young solder of *ill-fortune,*
Of an ache in his tum he complained
The timing was incredibly inopportune.

His appendix they grumbled we've had enough
In this army we're no longer stayin',
So they went *AWOL* during manoeuvres
Under operation *'Scalpel'* they went strayin'.

Not to be outdone William took umbrage
Couldn't be omitted from the equation,
He baffled the doctors with his symptoms
Last I heard he was under observation.

I think he goes into *theatre* today
What they'll find is only speculation,
It'll be no *pantomime* that's for sure
There will be *pain, boredom* and *humiliation.*

The moral of this saga is plain to see
When someone falls ill ~ *keep it quiet,*
For others might come out in sympathy,
It really is best not to try it.

George S Johnstone

The Boss

'Molly! Where's the paper clips? And where's me rubber stamp?
I've studied these figures so many times, me eyeball's got the cramp.

Now, where's the new typist gone again?
And look, me blotting paper's blue!
If the staff in this office wants a rise this year,
Well hard luck, you'll have to make do!

'Mrs Danks, me biscuits are broken, and me tea is nearly cold,
Another six months of you lot and I shan't live to be old!'

There's a mountain of bills sitting under me nose,
And me fountain pen's run out of ink,
And the sales rep must have been drunk last night,
The fool's been sick in the sink!

Give me my golf clubs, Lucinda, I'm going out for an hour,
There's going to be down-sizing when I get back,
I'm going to exercise me power!'

Anthony George Teesdale

Retirement

I thought that when I retired
Life would be slower, that *must*
Have been a dream I'd acquired.
My friends at the office used to say,
'You lucky old thing, no work every day.'
How little they know, they *will* have a shock!
Although there's no rush to live by the clock
But you still have a lot to get done
And these little jobs go *on* and *on*
There is all the shopping and cooking to do
Then washing and ironing, *still* there too.
Also I spend time at the surgery
Not that I enjoy that particular chore
I'd rather chat to my friend next door.
The two of us find places to go
More time together, or, go to a show.
No more dashing to work every week
We even find the time to speak!
Just me and my spouse,
Happily retired in our nice little house.

Betty Clark

A Holiday Time Rhyme

Summer holiday time ~ time to escape from it all
So we book our flight and pack our case
And we're off to the sea and the sun
We check the times of trains and flights
And we're off to enjoy the fun.
It's hard to get to the station because of the cars on the road
But still as usual the train is late
And we struggle with our luggage load.
Of course, no seats, so we have to stand
But arrive at the airport at last
We get checked in, but the flight is late
And our tummies say meal time's well past.
At last we make it on the plane ~
But the seats could be a lot better
But drinks from the well-stocked bar ~ well
They suit us to the letter.
At touchdown we think our troubles are o'er
But no coach to our choice of hotel
So we find our way as best we can
It seems like a journey to hell.
Next year we'll sit in our garden
Who cares if it sometimes rains?
We can put up our feet, sleep, eat and enjoy
Forget about coaches, planes, trains.
It might sound a little bit boring ~
To us it sounds heaven on earth
After this year's disaster
All things can be faced with much mirth.

Edna Wilcox

Waking World

When dawn's pale fingers reach across the sky,
retreating shadows leave their hazy trail.
A shrouded bough points out the reason why
night slowly lifts her dark, bemisted veil.
And yet, no stir of waking or of sound
while still the spreading pearl of light doth glow,
revealing peaceful pastures all around
and the river's lambent, silent flow.

The steeple of the little village church
emerges through the distant blur of trees.
Even the air is still, while oak and birch
await the rousing touch of summer breeze.
And then, the first clear note of song is heard
from a clump of fern with fronds yet unfurled.
Gentle at first then swelling, as a bird
calls out his welcome to the waking world.

Catherine Clough

I Love Him

My heart leaps at his voice,
In this I have no choice!
I love him.

He gets me through each day,
In his own special way.
I love him.

He keeps me whole and sane,
And takes away my pain.
I love him.

He loves me just for me,
I will eternally,
Love him.

Debbie Pawley

Cherry Blossom

Floating gently on the breeze
A'flutter in the sky
The soft and flimsy blossom
Goes sweetly gliding by.

It falls upon the dewy grass
Like snow upon the ground
Pink and white and beautiful
Without the merest sound.

It lasts but for a day or two
But what a wondrous sight
This blossom bursting on the trees
In the sunshine's glorious light.

For a moment or two it had its life
It shone like a bride in May
Blooming in all its beauty
And brightened our Springtime's day.

Mollie D Earl

Racking And Rocking

Racking and rocking through Switzerland
Scarves of mist where the mountains stand,
Narrow gauge railways constantly climbing,
Occasional glimpses of sun shining.

From Wilderswill to Schynige Platte
The wheels rock with unending chatter,
Festoons of wild flowers around us cast,
As we twist and turn, rising fast;

Scorning clouds, the Jungfrau appears,
Ermine clad, crowned with years.
From vast to tiny, a butterfly,
Emerald green hairstreak, flutters by.

Pouring rain from Brig to Zermatt,
Rack railway up the Gornergraat.
Views obscured by snow and rain,
Pause at a station, climbing again:

Alighting at the top my umbrella
Is transformed to a snow pagoda.
Glasses of Gluwein fortify
Our hearts for the return journey.

Bernina Express to bella Tirano,
Shadowy blue glaciers flecked with snow
Reflected in mountain lakes, while small
Geckos bask on a sun-drenched wall.

A boat on Lake Thun, weaving
Around the mountains' rocky roots,
Sweet benison of sunlight,
Embalmed in nature's silence:
The land's heart beating.

Elizabeth Aylward

75

A Rhyme In Time

Change the world they say
Why not change the day
Put evil at bay
And see where the goodness lay,

In time to make things mend
A hand we must so lend
It costs nothing to befriend.

Everybody can learn
Today we will adjourn
And show our own concern.

We have our human rights
Try to amuse not abuse
From the Sacred Cow to the Taj Mahal
To see the world of sights.

Have a reason for the season
Don't giggle or niggle, share your views,
Hoping it's good news.

S G White

You

You're always there for me,
Always there to care for me
I feel like I love you
Can't say 'I love you'
All I can do is feel for you
I feel like we've been through
So much in such our short time
Wanna spend my whole time with you
I'd forever miss you
If you'd ever leave me
Please, please don't ever leave
At times I feel like you're all I have
Nothing else to hold my life together
You're the only one to put a smile on my face.

Sarah L Grigor

Slow Dance

She turns to smile
and nails me through the
heart
holding me there almost breathless
with those dark eyes
her hands upon my shoulders
and I dread the moment when the music changes
and we shall have to move apart.

If only I could spend time sublime
marooned in that smile and the candlelight;
or feel those hands on my shoulders in the subdued
aura of a bedside lamp. I want her to arrest me; to feel
the wheel of my heart secured
by her tender clamp.

She talks, I listen
wanting to touch her face
and still those lips with a kiss,
exulting in this tortuous embrace.
But I listen ~ suspended by her beauty which
glistens night and day.

Desire ~ exhilarating and heady,
my hands resting on her waist as though
reality has fled me and fantasy permanently
taken its place. And yet her body is warm
and real enough as the music swirls all around us.
Slow dance in a shadowy banqueting hall,
her new dress shimmering white
her eyes and pale skin shining;
the touch and vision of her
filling me with a savage delight.

But the next day I wait
for the phone to ring or for the sight
of her face, the tone of her voice, the sound
of her name. I burn again for another embrace
but at the same time yearn to escape this searing
combination of pleasure and pain.

Tom Delaney

Sorcery

We walk in silence. Words would seem to be
Raucous voices in a house of prayer,
Hornets buzzing round a picnic tea.
When words are banished, silence leaves me free
To notice many things that in the past
My eyes had seen although my brain had not;
To be aware of sounds my ears had heard
Of which my conscious mind was unaware.

Does this silence work for everyone
Or operate for only me with I'm with you?
What is this magic power you generate?
Why does it work its potent spell on me?
Perhaps it's not so hard to understand.
I think I've known the culprit all along.
It's down to that old Devil they call Love.
Strange I have not rumbled him till now!

Kathleen McGowan

When Love Dies

He put her on a pedestal
Now he puts her on the floor
The things he does, the things he says
It wasn't like that before.
He used to say he loved her
That they would never part
But now everything has changed.
He doesn't care if he breaks her heart.
She stares into space thinking
What she should do.
Wonders if it's possible to start anew.
Tear-stained cheek, pain-filled heart
She knows now they are better off apart.
Perhaps it was never meant to last
Their love is finally a thing of the past.

Sheila Western

Unrequited Love

What task can I perform, to show my love for you?
Shall I get up at sunrise, and collect the morning dew
As a token of the tears that I have shed, because of you.
Or wait until the stars come out, and fill the sky with light.
Then gather them in baskets, 'til there isn't one in sight
As a token of the brightness that I see when you are near.
But even though I do these things, I can't make you love me, dear.

Amelia Wilson

More Than This

I need you ~
As much as the sky needs the stars
And the sea needs the water,
But even more than this ~
For without you
I cease to exist.

I live only to see you
Speak to you and touch you,
But even more than this ~
To feel your warmth
And the softness and strength of your body.

My need for you
Is greater than the whole world,
For you are my eyes and my mind,
But even more than this ~
You are my knowledge
And everything that I'll ever know.

Without you nothing else matters
Least of all myself,
For I am part of you
And when your love for me dies
I will die also.

Gillian Berry

My First Love

I was just eleven
When I met the man for me,
He was five years older
And as handsome as can be.
He'd come to stay from London
With his cousin for the summer,
And my best friend and me
Were struck by love ~ like dumb and dumber!
We waited for him after work
So we could catch a glance,
Both of us knew well
That we would never stand a chance.
We listened to old love songs
As we sat upon my bed,
Both wishing he'd be ours
As all the countless tears we shed.
The more we got to know him
The deeper we would fall,
Until the pair of us
Could think of nothing else at all.
And then the day we'd dreaded came,
Our Phil was going home,
For months we wrote him poems, letters
Stayed in all alone.
But then we met some other boys
Who took our minds off Phil,
But even now occasionally
I wonder about him still.

Laura Berry

84

False Friend

When first we two did meet,
It seemed you understood.
You woke my heart again
As no-one else could.
The months went slowly by,
And still you lit my way.
I thought our paths would lie
Along the self-same way.
You made belief by words
So sweet and tenderly said.
You thought the world of me,
But sadly, you misled.
For words are empty things,
If be not really true.
False Friend, you are unkind,
In thoughtless acts you do.
Speak not with forked tongue,
But straight from out your heart.
The world will better be,
If you'll but play your part!

Dorothy Ventris

My 'Karma' The Afghan

My dearest and most loving friend
Whose race was known 5000 years BC
Is lying in a sphinx position
With his golden mysterious eyes watching me.

His coat is long, soft, silky and fair
Gently moving in the breeze
Like a leaf in the morning air.

He knew every movement of mine
He knew whether it was going to rain, or be fine.
He loved to roam the hilltops, run on the seashore
But most of all, travel in the car.

His vocabulary was fantastic as well
If I did not want him to understand
I had to spell.

He was human, or should I say, as humans should be?
I knew and always felt his love for me.
But then he too knew I loved him
For as his servant I looked after his every whim.

I did not own him, but he owned me,
If one understands the word Karma, one can see.
That he lived up to his name and left his presence behind
Like a golden flame.

Erika Rollinson

If Only

If only I had met you in another space in time.
The years could have rolled back,
And I could have made you mine.
Destiny is the strangest thing,
It complicates our hearts,
Because you and I can never be,
We shall always be apart.
The gap between us is too wide,
You'll live on long after I'll have died.
In the meantime I'll just dream,
And fantasise what could have been.

Eileen Patricia Dunn

Adam

I shiver at his touch, watch in fascination
As his hands caress my skin
Wanting him so badly
Surely has to be a sin

I have only one thought, he steals my mind
Only three words, do I know
I need you, I love you
And please don't go!

I hold my breath, to stop the time
I still my heart, to hear his beating
There is no other sound,
As skin to skin our souls are meeting

Joan Wright

Ode To Love

Alright my master?
Alright my queen?

For this was the case of the sax verses the violin, the windband versus
the orchestra,
The pink panther and the marriage of Figaro versus hymns and arias
The mellow hybrid tones of the sax versus clear path of violins
and cellos.

She would sit in nylons full of dignity, composed
Whilst I had my view awide from the back of the audience
Nothing daring made the picture complete
A pose of calm and moment making her beauty translucent.

Valentines I sent and those acknowledged led
To her gentle touch and kisses once with a broken arm
Love letters were read out but my musical prowess was to turn her off
As it could never be reciprocated and she became aloof.

Every girl who came later was to compare with this one
They had to have a very strong will indeed
For they felt the stone of indifference if they had emotion
To mend my ways in time to do is what I shall need.

I have too much respect for the businesswoman and law practitioner.
Like-minded females I tend to ignore
My last girlfriend was a short-lived pleasure
She charmed me with the beating hearts of the hairdresser.

I can smile with radiance at her past deception
For her trust was never with me and my heart pained
Now I sing in small places and focus the radio on jazz
Whilst my school fave is miles away, with a husband to send
her flowers.

David Lloyd

Grace

How can You say You love us
When we've got it so very badly wrong?
~ And yet You do!
You love us so much
You came to save us
If we just
Turn to You.

I see injustice
And I hate it
But then
So do You . . .

Thousands of sacred cows
Yet thousands of starving people . . .

Land regeneration into ¼ million pound flats
And yet many people
Can't afford to pay their rent
Or don't have a job . . .

Muslim women locked up in houses
Or enshrouded behind a veil . . .

And yet the Lord longs
To be gracious to you,
O nations.
Why don't you turn
And see Jesus' way:
Loving, forgiving ~
Nothing else matters.

Natalie Jagger

The Dewdrop Inn
(Based on a pub in the county of Worcestershire)

Hidden from view by the cobweb dew,
And the early morning mist.
Staggering along the country lane,
Old Bill, starboard list.
On remote control through the gate,
Old Bill, he's never late.
The Dewdrop Inn with open doors,
With creaking oak boards on the floor.
And tables which have seen better days,
With moonshine drinkers and full ash trays.
To enter the Dewdrop Inn beware,
For the moonshine drinkers just don't care.
There is easy rider at the bar,
While lady breaker smokes his fat cigar.
Serving the tables with a big fat grin,
Is old slack Alice with a double gin.
Leaning over tables low,
Everything hangs out on show.
A gentle brush, a big heave to,
Old Alice says, 'I got room for you.'
Frightened to death I approached the bar,
And ordered my moonshine from the jar.
A quick sip and I couldn't move a limb,
I thought, I wish I'd stuck to the bloody gin.
Another sip, and I couldn't speak,
I couldn't move my bloody feet.
Locked in an armlock around the bar,
Sat old Bill with his moonshine jar.
Staggering I was helped out the door,
Starboard listing I heard the call.
'What the bloody hell, you've been drinking,'
I retorted, 'Shut your mouth, I'm thinking.'
The time was only 10am, it was Sunday,
That was when I remembered, I'm vicar Grundy.

John Hickman

91

Me 'N' Jesus

Spent the day walkin' round the town.
Hands in my pockets trying hard to hide my frown.
Sun shining high, there's not a cloud in sight,
Somethin's been bugging me, kept me awake all night,
Gotta get myself a job and stop feeling used,
Gonna call a special friend who wears the holy shoes.

Jesus is my friend and I want you to know,
He gave a helping hand and made the good times flow.

Me 'n' Jesus went for a swim,
He told me that He'd save me if I ever fell in.
Me 'n' Jesus went for a walk,
He told me He would listen if I needed to talk,
And me 'n' Jesus hung out for a while,
We really had a good time, had a 'halo'va time.

Jesus is my pal, yeah you need to know,
He knew just what to do when I was feeling low.

Me 'n' Jesus went to town to a pub,
Drank some holy water, ended up in a club,
Yeah me 'n' Jesus partied right through the night,
Drinking and getting down until the morning light,
Then me 'n' Jesus stopped to eat a kebab,
Time to hit the road so we hailed down a cab.

Jesus is my friend Yeah He's your friend too,
He knows just what to do, He's got time for you.
When you're feeling down and you don't know what to do,
He will call around and change it all for you . . .

Stephen Owen

Contradictions!

Are you fastidious, lazy, excitable?
Someone who avoids decisions,
As well as paperwork.
Re-active yet evasive?
Does your mind switch off or smoulder?
When is it a day for positive action 'now'.
Do you live in a clutter,
Yet look spruced neat 'out and about'
Are you easily led
Or do you strongly hold your own?
A poor listener and a chatterbox,
Full of hot air and opinions!
A DIY fanatic or creative genius,
'Sporty' inclinations or an armchair traveller?
The foibles of being human
~ We are all 'one-offs'.

Margaret Ann Wheatley

Dreams

(This poem is dedicated to the girl of my dreams,
Sue Nicholson, Chris XXX)

Girl of my dreams
won't you come true for me,
make my life complete
open my eyes so I can see
the beauty that stands before me.

I see you every single night
but you're not really there,
I hear you call my name
you sound like a thousand angels singing
I hear you and I have to stand and stare.

You're there in my dreams
but why can't you be real,
put your hand on my heart
then you'll know how I feel,
when I am awake I miss your tender touch.

In my dreams you have the sweetest kiss
you have a smile that could light up the world,
the way you hold me makes my heart pound
I would move mountains to be with you,
I would do anything just to make my dreams come true.

Heaven could grow dark
and hell could freeze over,
that wouldn't mean a thing
just as long as I could have
the girl of my dreams.

Chris Barber

I 'Wanna-Be' A Grown-Up

I 'Wanna-be' a grown-up and have lots and lots of fun,
and never ever go to school but stay out in the sun;
I'd swim and play, eat sweets all day, and get home after ten
and stay in bed all morning ~ then do it all again.

I'm fed up being told I'm young and what I mustn't do,
I want to please myself a bit and let folk know 'who's who'
if shopping was my fancy, I'd spend and spend and spend,
till all my credit cards wore out ~ then use Dad's 'Flexi-friend'.

I'd wear my oldest clothes all day and never clean my shoes
or tidy up my bedroom or watch the rotten news,
I would *never* visit aunties except at *their* request
and if I didn't want to go again ~ I'd make myself a pest.

I'd sit and read a naughty book with my radio full blast,
then when I'd had enough of that, I'd watch the girls go past,
maybe I'll turn the 'telly' on and doze like grown-ups do
then phone out for a pizza, or better still ~ have two.

I'd travel all around the world to ski or chase the sun
then check in on the Internet to see how shares have done;
occasionally I'd come back home, but should it start to rain ~
I'd hop back on my 'Private Jet' to Portugal or Spain.

This thinking makes me hungry ~ 'Mum what is there for tea,
oh! ~ have you got my football shirt and boots you promised me,
Dad ~ will you take me in the car, and collect another two
I'll take your mobile phone along then ring when we are through.'

Oh! Dear ~ I've just remembered, today they work till nine,
I ought to tidy up this room then maybe start on mine;
I've heard them say it's work all day and very little pleasure
I'll just forget this 'Wanna-be' and stay *their* 'Little Treasure'.

Jim Pritchard

It's All Go

One always wants to be fair
Filling in that questionnaire
It is necessary to inform
Decide what type of uniform
Something not to arouse
Simple fitting shirt or blouse
Will not be a surprise
If one has the right size
Sensible colour or type
Choice of plain or stripe
Notepaper, pen or docket
Need for a large pocket
Bits and pieces to go on file
Got to be with style
Fashionable, sweat or tee shirt
To match with tapered jeans or skirt
One piece overall in packs
Failing that, straight slacks
What to do, Oh brother
Pick out the inevitable colour
Enough to make one scream
You've got blue, red or green
Black or gold to go
Two sets of clothing with the firm's logo
On foot or drive if you can
All we need now is a company van

Anthony Higgins

96

The Games Of The Old

Excuse me, what did you say?
I have this problem, of not hearing well,
deaf? Certainly not, you are
standing too far away from me, that's all!

Memory? Ah, my dear, I can remember in 1942 ~
what's that? I forgot your birthday last week?
Don't be silly, it's this weekend, oh, I must
remember to see Elsie tomorrow ~ we're playing cards.

No thanks, that cake is far too big for me, but you
wrap it up, I'll take it home, as the cat and I
will enjoy it, we only have each other for company.
No thanks, I don't want to sit in the car, while you go shopping,
cheek!

I wouldn't like to put you out, son, I know you and Lynne
are busy, oh yes, my knees are playing up ~ but don't worry,
I can ask Bert, next door, who's older than me, to water
my plants, and have a bit of cake with me ~ better not get any ideas!

Doctor next week ~ more tablets ~ such a nice man
I can get the bus, don't worry ~ have you and your mate made up?
You ought to sell that car ~ I don't like the colour;
You'll see, you'll be old ~ one day. It comes to all of us!

All the young people today, seem too busy, spending money,
and when they run out ~ they go on the dole!
Didn't have it in my day ~ and all those little phones,
why don't they just use BT ~ instead of oranges?

What's a people carrier? Cars carry people, don't they?
Some stupid woman, asked me if would deliver leaflets
for the aged! Cheek, told her I was old, and want charity.
Partners? Elsie is my partner ~ does that make me gay?

Diana Beck-Martin

When We Were Ready

A forest dense, paths interacting,
choices made on instinct pure.
Sunlight sparkle, following shadows,
a maze of visions tangled lure.

Compass points that have no meaning,
each direction a wishing-well
of hopes and joys and inspirations,
only fate and time could tell.

Deep in the thicket, caught on sorrow,
fighting free, the call is heard.
Lessons learnt, packed in their cases,
drag it through that muddy curve.

Life's lessons learnt, thought once a burden,
now needed for that hope and joy.
Life took me on this path to find you,
when we were ready ~ and not before.

Jeanette Clinton

Summer

God's summer garden radiates happiness and bliss

It makes one realise, right in front of
one's eyes, how the season of summer
gently and softly unfolds.
With spectacular cascades and displays
of pinks, lavenders and gold.
God in His glory reigned supreme.
And He gives us the soothing, calming
colours of green.
God in His glory and love did create
Flowers where the insects congregate ~
God's love is in the flowers and the
refreshing sun showers.
And His enchanting floral magic powers.

One can't help but admire the lovely
blue Canterbury bells, standing tall
and proud, so perfect and divine.
Which floods my heart with deep
emotion, and surely is a sign.
God's love is everywhere, and how
happy to have the privilege of
enjoying the perfection of summer's
dazzling bonanza of colour, and I
gaze with awe and wonder
at the beautiful heavenly blue of
'Love in the Mist'
knowing by the sun it has
been kissed.

Elizabeth Myra Crellin

Summertime

It's summertime once again,
The trees are in full bloom,
The sun shines through the window,
And brightens up the room.

The park is filled with children,
So happy are they at play,
The mothers enjoy the sunshine,
It drives their cares away.

The beaches at the seaside,
Are packed with families,
All enjoying their holidays,
In a happy mood and free.

The summertime gives us a chance,
To forget the winter blues,
So just enjoy its beauty,
With all its glorious hues.

The longer days and shorter nights
Are a bonus in itself,
It makes us feel much healthier,
And happier in ourselves.

So take advantage of this time,
And enjoy the summer sun,
For when you feel its warmth on you,
You'll really feel that summer has begun.

For there are many things taking place,
During the summer months,
Like flower shows and festivals
And ferry cruises too.

Don't stay in the house all day
Go out and enjoy the sun,
For there are plenty of things to do,
Go out and have some fun.

Joan Haworth

A Winter's Tail

When the wily fox of winter,
Leaves his tracks across your way,
Does he realise it's Christmas,
Or is it just another day.

All safe beside our fires,
With food enough to eat,
He walks a lonely hedgerow,
Through wind and snow and sleet.

Hounded by the huntsman,
And the farmer with his gun,
All alone at Christmas,
Forever on the run.

When the wily fox of winter,
Leaves his tracks across your way,
Cold and hunger stalk him,
It is just another day.

Allan Wood

Mummy Is . . .

Mummy is very happy,
And she buys lots of nappies.
Mummy is a bright star,
She gets more and more.
Mummy is what she wants to be,
But she doesn't like swimming in the sea.
Mummy is kind,
She's got peace of mind.
Mummy is calm,
She would never harm.
Mummy is polite,
She kisses me goodnight.
Mummy is tidy,
Today it's Friday.
Mummy is a whiz kid!

Jessica Jepson (7)

My Children

A trio of faces smiling up at me,
Not a better sight a mother could see,
You three are what makes my world go round,
I love you all dearly, my love is so profound,
What beautiful miracles of nature you are,
Who could ask for any more,
A bond so strong and true,
Holds all the love I have for you,
My heart swells with pride,
When I have you all by my side,
I am so very lucky you see,
For you three were chosen just for me,
So thank you for all the joy and happiness,
That has enriched all our lives,
Three special children, that's what you are,
Mine to cherish forever more.

Andrea M Jepson

My Love For You

When I met you
You awakened something in me
I never knew existed
Love I'd always resisted
I was too scared and shy
To show my feeling to anyone till I met you
You showed me what life and love was all about
No-one can replace you in my heart
Of that there is no doubt
You weren't *just* my husband 'Albert'
You were my 'lover' my best 'friend'
I thought it would never end
But it did
And a part of me died with you

Margaret Toft

To Jimmy

You had a dog, Rex was his name,
He ran away from me, I was to blame,
I dressed him in a bonnet of lace,
And put him in a nice warm place,
But he jumped out of my doll's pram,
Down the back entry, he ran,
After him I followed, to retrieve my lace bonnet,
Only to find it abandoned, with dirt upon it.

I had a dog, Lady was her name,
She broke her leg, it left her lame,
She sat all day long on a cushion of lace,
And I kept her warm, in a nice warm place,
Sadly her long life came to an end,
And that's when I lost my very best friend,
So made her a bed of satin and lace,
And I keep her close by, in her own special place.

Jean-Ruth Coleman

Psalm 23 My Shepherd Is Love's Lord

At the rushes' edge love saw me,
To green fields love bore me.

By a clear brook love took me,
On a grassy path love put me.

Love spoke and it was true:
Your life I will renew.

Death shadows all my ways,
But love guards all my days.

Before all who hate me,
Love sets a feast to fête me.

Love's grace is life's gain,
Bringing joy removing pain.

I'll lodge with love all my days,
Give to God all my praise.

Derek Webster

A Lonely Planet's Mountain
(For Jim and Joss)

Today I've climbed my mountain and there's no place else I'd be
I'm sitting here with Maslow drinking actualisation tea.
What a glorious perspective, worries distant and so small
Up here I'm free to be myself, to stand up proud and tall.
This cool crisp air it bites me, and wakes me up to life
I fill my lungs and cleanse my soul and step down off the knife.
Rarely do I climb so high, that I can touch the sun
I'm basking in its warmth and love, I'll stay here till it's done.
When this splendid sun sets, my joy will not be barred
For then I'll spend an evening with a host of glittering stars.
No cable-cars, no tourists, this Mountain belongs to me
Here I have my answers, I'm all that I can be.
I look back past my shoulder to see a wondrous sight
A hundred other Mountains, making up my light
On one I see six young men, black tie and Tootal joy
Amongst them is a giant, a developing young boy.
Waving from my Mountain I want to cry and shout
Today is what I live for, what life is all about.
And when it's time to go and I'm back down in the sea
I'll close my eyes and think of now, I know I'll taste the tea.
For this Mountain will be a castle, in a beautiful blue green land
Filled with an inspirational love, standing hand in hand.
The Castle's name is Pride and today I am the king
Thank you man and wife to be, you've made my heart sing.

Lance Bennett

My Mind's Eye

I often look up at the sky
And watch the clouds drifting by,
Some quite huge ~ others small
Sometimes they hardly move at all.
I see pictures in my mind's eye
As they slowly pass on by,
Some so large they look like creatures
Like Dinosaurs in TV features,
Others look like geese in flight ~
Or swans floating on a lake of blue,
And groups of high white mountains too,
A pretty lagoon surrounded by trees
Sometimes a ship upon calm seas,
Some are shaped like ancient castles ~
Surrounded by groups of isles ~
Even shapes of human faces
Looking down with a happy smile,
A band of angels with outstretched wings
What peace of mind this do bring,
White horses too in galloping stride
Such wonderful pictures in my mind's eye.

Olive Godfrey

To The Sparrows Who Flew Away

Why did the sparrows fly away?
Where did they go?
Now I am able to tell you.
Lured by the call of Zeus
They flew to ancient Greece,
With its clear blue skies
And deeper blue seas
Its sunshine and olive trees.
Welcome, welcome little birds,
Smiled the Gods from their mountain tops.
Twitter and tweet for our delight.
Come and live with us.
The sparrows thought of the land they had left,
With its steel grey skies and endless cold rain
And nowhere left to live.
Thank you, they said.
We will stay here
In this beautiful land of yours.
And forgetting the land they had left,
Happy birds,
That's exactly what they did.
What more could a sparrow require?

Marian Rutland

The Beating Heart

So regular, is, the beating heart.
When, all in life, is well.
Like, the beating, of, a watch, or clock.
Its pace, a tale, will tell.

The speeding of the beating heart
To young ones, in, true love.
The slowness of, the ageing hearts
When all, in life's, not well.

Our hearts, show, mixed emotions.
Expressions of, the face.

An inner clock, that shows, to all
Its irregularity, of pace.

Our hearts, show all, our happiness.
Our hearts, show all, our peace.
Our hearts, show all, our sadness
By its constant rhythmic beat.

Leslie Rushbury

My Secret Place

My name is darling Sophie and I'm only just turned 3
There are fairies at the bottom of my garden
Which only I can see
They live in a beautiful toadstool
Which they sprinkle with silver and gold
So when I go there to see them
I really must do as I'm told
And they only come out to see me
And dance for me over the dew
If I promise to keep this my secret
And not even share it with you.

Jean Myhill

Natalie, Jacob And Joseph

Two boys and one girl, you'd think there was an army.
Am I going mad, no, just slightly barmy.
There's wild animals in the bath and felt tips on their face,
With worms in the garage ~ they're observing?
    No having a race.

Cover the table and the three-piece
Move all the tablets, the treasures and the keys.
Bathtime's a fiasco with water to the top
One little boy remarks that the girl's must have dropped off!

Bedtime at last ~ peace ~ oh no not yet
There's springs creaking, faces peeping, drinks and scary pets
It's tiring and hard work but there's so much joy
They're monsters? No just our grandchildren
    One girl and two little boys.

Betty Gordon